Hitchhiking with...

Copyright © Nick Voro 2024

All rights reserved. No part of this publication may be reproduced or transmitted in any form or by any means, electronic or mechanical, including photocopying, recording, or any information storage and retrieval system, without permission in writing from the publisher.

First Edition

Hitchhiking with...

VoroBooks, Etobicoke, Ontario, Canada

ISBN: 978-1-7383199-7-8

Typesetting and additional design by Lee Thompson Editing+

To contact the author: Nick_Voro@hotmail.com

This is a work of fiction. Names, characters, places and incidents either are products of the author's imagination or are used fictitiously. Any resemblance to actual events or locales or persons, living or dead, is entirely coincidental.

HITCHHIKING WITH...

SOMEHOW, WE MISSED IT. When we eventually became aware of its existence and trajectory it was too late. It shook our deeply-embedded trust in world leaders, the armed forces and the navy, bespectacled scientists, and the astronomers responsible for the President's Aeronautics and Space reports.

It sent people scattering, whimpering, unprepared to deal with such a cataclysmic event. When

Conversational Therapy

it hit, its force caused mass destruction, the complete cessation of normality, and relented only slightly in the end, as if acquiring enough conscience to spare a few for preservation of human life on this planet.

Natural selection prevailed, few became fewer, long-standing rivalries resulted in segregation and formation of warring parties, retrogression, collapse of unity, allegiances pledged and further formation of fractious factions giving way to unpardonable imbecility, erratic behavior and irrationality of thought. War enveloped the land, dead covered the soil like scattered grains, everything engulfed in flames, primordial combat depleting natural resources and causing widespread famine; until one day the implacable war, with no resolution in sight, finally ended. Next came a period of catharsis, with the strongest war party issuing a respite to all who joined them. A great proliferation to their numbers, selling dreams, promises, splendorous possibilities, all the while subjugating, brainwashing, clinching the submissiveness of their followers with a non-negotiable contract (the real price of the membership) legally binding them and their offspring(s) for life.

The vanquished non-conformists remained resolute, refusing to join the others (those blind bootlickers incapable of reclaiming their natural rights), deciding to continue living in the old, abandoned cities, enduring intolerable conditions, deprived of manpower and tools necessary for organic progression and forever fugitives in the eyes of those victors who left and went on to form the New World Order. This ruinous state housing the outcasts came to be known as the Human Zone.

Which is where you find yourself, cognizant of the fact you should not be here, knowing well the consequences of capture for anyone illegally crossing into the Human Zone. Especially a reporter with a camera, an apparatus capable of capturing what the New World Order has worked so hard to destroy, the Zone a smear on their

Conversational Therapy

painstakingly perfected world.

Their aim is to erase everything that has come before their cherished Utopia. To rewrite history without mentioning the past.

When you were younger, you used to say you were no different from a journalist going out of his way to get to the facts. Now you are one. The right career for someone with a quizzical mindset and a lifelong infatuation with discovering, in the ruins of the past, the book outlining creation itself, a book as old as time itself—the Holy Bible. This obsession with the past is what brings you here today.

Ironically enough, for a desolate place, you encounter someone almost straight away. A single car approaches (a baffling sight, a relic of the past completely restored and in working order). A car! You had wondered how many were still around. Not thinking, as if this is how it should be, sticking out your thumb, you make the car slow down. You ask for a lift. When queried about your destination by the Driver, you reply vaguely, "I wish I knew."

Hitchhiking with...

"Get in. You can figure it out along the way." He waits until you get inside before continuing. "You aren't from around here," he says, keeping his eyes studiously forward, such stern concentration seeming excessive to you, considering the solitary vehicle on a deserted road like this.

"That obvious, eh?"

"What brings you out here?"

You look at him, then at the darting landscape through the pristine window of a car long presumed lost to a world that is no more. "Rummaging."

"Is that what you do in the place you come from; you rummage?"

"You could say that. I am a journalist for one of the large corporations. Just out here rummaging for facts."

"The New World Order has all the facts they need. They do not come here. They stay out. Steer clear. Which makes me think you aren't supposed to be here."

"I am not."

Conversational Therapy

"Facts... about...?"

You cannot help but notice a crucifix, gold—now such a worthless metal—hanging from his rear-view mirror. "Our origins."

"Well, son, we are all children of the same father. The Holy Father."

"Opinions may vary."

"What do you mean?" he says and looks at you, clearly the most blasphemous heathen he has ever met in his life.

"Very few people know this place even exists. Call it convenient forgetfulness, a memory lapse, or lack of traditionalist storytelling from person to person, but they never talk about the past, what transpired before. They live their lives in the present with thoughts only about the future."

"But not you."

"No. Not me. I am a logician. A researcher. When the World Leader told me nothing existed before the New World Order came to be, I did not buy it. Mind you, he was really going for it. The hard sell. He was his usual self, personable and undeniably magnetic, I will give him that. Our beloved World Leader really tried to win me over. He even brandished an advance copy of the New World Testament to strengthen his point."

"The what…"

"Revisionist history from the self-appointed World Leader."

"He wrote his own bible?"

"Everyone's forgotten about the Old and the New Testament, blindly wringing their hands before a false prophet fearing jail, public denouncement or worse yet, *beheading* by the leader's own creation, one formerly discovered and named after its inventor, Joseph-Ignace Guillotin."

"This is most unnatural," he says, strangulating the steering wheel with tension-riddled hands.

"What can one expect from a man who crowned himself creator and ruler at his own coronation, placed the crown atop his own head. Since then, he has been burying the past, burying everything that preceded his reign."

Conversational Therapy

"So, he thinks God, or His son Jesus Christ are…"

"A pair of fictional characters. Part of a made-believe world. Not his world. Not his reality."

"And what about you, son, what do you believe?" He turns halfway toward you.

His interest is apparent, and your answer presents some issues as a non-believer. "I am somewhat on the cusp."

"What scares me is not one nonbeliever in Christ, but millions of people who idolize a… a dictator."

"His ambition knows no limits."

"He would be selling his soul to the Devil if he were to go through with the publication."

"The Devil to him is just a minor reoccurring character in what used to be a bestseller."

"If that book is made available to the masses, he will… un-make the world."

"Un-make?"

"A greedy man with an inimical gaze coveting

imperial sovereignty will open the floodgates."

"The flood of Genesis?"

He gestures toward the sky. "The comet was just a warning for what's to come."

"If that were a warning, I would hate to see the imminent hazard we are being warned about. The world cannot handle another disaster."

"You are right, the world would not recover. I repeat, if that book comes out, forget about expiation, expect only the end, the death of the human race. And the suffering will be immense…" He turns to you, and you cannot help but notice the passion in his eyes. "Imagine! One man, mortal human tissue, flesh and blood like you and me, inundating the world with his… his distended ego, his distortions, enacting a false prophet's prophecy attempting to shatter mankind's unbreakable bond; and the people trading devotion to the Lord for idolization of an evil entity simply because they don't know any better. Deprived of the most accurate record of creation—God's very own heavenly blueprints—to reference and guide

Conversational Therapy

them in their lives. These same blueprints, which detail the origins of humanity, the birthing of intelligent life with cognitive abilities necessary for greatest possible progression. An account of humanity's preservation, the planting of seeds of knowledge, the ability to construct with basic tools, and using those simple stone implements to build their own world with, tools that sadly turned into weapons with time and innovation, weapons used to commit murder of their fellow men, weapons used to kill the son of God, the child of the master builder, creator of all life on earth. And now your leader wants to hide historical truth from the world, keep hidden the work of God's chosen transcriptionists, scribes in charge of transcribing his miracles with ink on papyrus, preserving the history of humanity's origins. He wants to conceal the truth, hide a book detailing the divine ruler's divine creation. Offering instead a substitution and imposing on mankind his book of falsities as absolute truth."

"Are you a preacher?"

Hitchhiking with...

"I used to be, but what I remain is a believer."

Silence shrouded the rest of the ride. Eventually you asked him to pull over. This deserted stretch looked as good a place as any.

A period of pondering and wandering the Human Zone followed until your return to the world on the other side, the progressive world, where you proceeded to wallow in uncertainty until one fated night you decide to act. This was the day before the World Leader was to release his own re-telling of the world.

Disguised, you distribute your unsigned pamphlet solely underground under the title, "Hitchhiking with Jesus." Even after writing, handing out and depleting your stock you remain plagued with doubt. Were you the envoy of Christ, or a mouthpiece for a lunatic? Your words, the story you told, ignited the gunpowder, issuing a challenge to the dictator presiding over a dystopian government. And while you remained uncertain,

Conversational Therapy

the people decided for themselves. They spoke the words you wrote. The words you heard uttered in your presence. They chanted these words. They became a form of prayer. The pamphlet became a bible. Words written there seen as scripture. The Warning as punishment for breaking a holy commandment. They reformed their views in accordance to the pamphlet. Pledged to reform their entire lives once they effected a change. But social change like this could only come through blood. Riots broke out, a revolution took place, the World Leader was first dethroned and later assassinated by a member of his close-knit circle of advisers. His book never did see the light of day. All copies were collected and incinerated. There were no more World Leaders for a long while. Oddly enough, you received a promotion, position of restorer of sacred texts, restoring the two editions of the Bible from what scraps of information you could locate hidden in the home of the former World Leader. When you published your efforts that winter, The New World Order seized

Hitchhiking with...

to exist, officially dismantled, giving rise to new parties and leadership. The mysterious preacher never did say which world would end.

ABOUT THE AUTHOR

A native of Kyiv, Ukraine, but living in Canada since the age of eleven, Nick Voro discovered literature at an early age, never quite mustering the ability to put an excellent book down. A recent graduate of the Toronto Film School, Nick divides his time between being a full-time parent and a full-time author.

His debut work, *Conversational Therapy: Stories and Plays*, has recently sold over 200 copies and is part of the library system (United States, Canada, New Zealand, Australia and Scotland).

Lee D. Thompson, an editor and writer from Moncton, New Brunswick, Canada, edited this short story. His books include: a novel in [xxx] dreams from Broken Jaw Press, Mouth Human Must Die from Frog Hollow Press and Apastoral: A Mistopia from Corona/Samizdat. His short fiction has been published in many anthologies, including Random House's Victory Meat, New Fiction from Atlantic Canada and Vagrant Press's The Vagrant Revue of New Fiction. He is the winner of the David Adams Richards Prize (2018) and New Brunswick Book Award (2022). He is the publisher of Galleon Books.

www.ingramcontent.com/pod-product-compliance
Lightning Source LLC
Chambersburg PA
CBHW030536080526
44585CB00014B/971